**Editorial Project Manager**
Lorin E. Klistoff, M.A.

**Managing Editors**
Karen Goldfluss, M.S. Ed.
Ina Levin, M.S. Ed.

**Illustrator**
Renée Christine Yates

**Cover Artist**
Barb Lorseyedi

**Art Production Manager**
Kevin Barnes

**Imaging**
James Edward Grace

**Publisher**
Mary D. Smith, M.S. Ed.

# Dr. Fry's
## Reading Activities
### Grades 2–3 · Full Color

**Author**

*Edward Fry, Ph.D.*

Teacher Created Resources

*Teacher Created Resources, Inc.*
6421 Industry Way
Westminster, CA 92683
www.teachercreated.com
**ISBN-1-4206-3150-0**
©2006 Teacher Created Resources, Inc.
Made in U.S.A.

# Table of Contents

# Introduction

The full-color reading activities in this book are designed to reinforce reading skills. Classroom teachers, reading teachers, and special education teachers will all find these materials beneficial to their students. The activities can be used to supplement any reading program and other commerical materials. Many of the activities can be used in language arts centers. The materials and/or directions can be laminated so they can be reused.

The first part of the book begins with several teaching ideas for reading. Next, a phonics activity is introduced. Students practice identifying the correct diphthongs, digraphs, or other vowel sounds for various words.

To help students decode unknown words, included is an activity dealing with word parts. The word parts include prefixes, suffixes, Greek roots, and Latin roots.

The next part of the book includes activities using stories. The first activity uses stories to teach homophones, synonyms, and antonyms. The second story activity involves story starters to help students write their own stories. The last story activity focuses on comprehension by having students answer questions from a story card.

The last part of the book reinforces the Instant Words. Dr. Fry's Instant Word list comprises the most important words for reading and writing in the English language. It is absolutely impossible to read or write anything without knowing at least some of these words. This book contains activities for teaching Instant Words 151–300. Whether through a pairs card game or a board game, students will learn the Instant Words that compose a high percentage of all reading material.

Students also can use the Picture Nouns and Instant Words Charts which are located at the end of the book to help support the activities included in this book.

For more practice with Dr. Fry materials, there are two companion books which cover the other Instant Words and Picture Nouns. TCR 3148 full-color *Dr. Fry's Reading Activities* (Grades K–1) covers Instant Words 1–50 and TCR 3149 full-color *Dr. Fry's Reading Activities* (Grades 1–2) covers Instant Words 51–150. Picture Noun cards located in these two books can be used with the Picture Noun reference chart on page 171.

# Teaching Ideas

- Read to students every day!

- Include drama (plays) for oral reading, speaking, and listening experiences.

- Write a story developed by your students on a large sheet of paper. Save and read later or at the end of a week.

- Have students write every day. For example, have them keep a journal or diary, write summaries of what they have read, or write a letter to a friend.

- Set a good example by reading often and encouraging parents to do the same.

- Use graphic organizers, like a time line for history or directions, a flow chart of a story, or a cluster of characteristics associated with a vocabulary word.

- Have students use computers for story writing.

- Encourage students to join a book club.

- Try using a captioned television to teach reading.

- Have students read the same story over and over again, not just until oral errors disappear but until reasonable speed and fluency appear.

- Emphasize comprehension. Form questions before reading, during, and after reading. Ask the students to recall, summarize, and compare.

- Get a joke book. Read one a day. Joke books or joke columns in newspapers and magazines make entertaining reading for children.

- Develop background knowledge about a reading selection. Talk about the setting, the characters, similar circumstances, or similar subject matter.

- Expand students' vocabulary any way you can: by reading, speaking, and picking words out of reading selections and discussing them.

- Make time for students to read for pleasure.

- Have students read different materials such as a booklet, directions for assembling a toy, lyrics from a popular song, short poems, post office forms, local maps, or bus schedules.

- Find out what subjects your students are interested in by making an interest inventory for students, or use the lesson on story starters on page 63.

# Same Sounds

## Skill

- Students identify the correct diphthong, digraph, or other vowel sound for each word.

## Grouping

- independent
- pairs
- small group

## Materials

- one of the following charts and cards:

  AI or AY? (page 7)   ER, IR, or UR? (page 13)   OU or OW? (page 19)

  AL, AU, or AW? (page 9)   OA or OW? (page 15)

  EA or EE? (page 11)   OI or OY? (page 17)

- writing utensils
- scissors
- multiple copies of My Words (page 6)
- Answer Key for "Same Sounds" (page 21)

## Directions

1. Pick one of the charts and cards with which to work. (*Note*: Make mulitple copies if you want to work with a large group.)
2. Cut out the word parts at the bottom of the page.
3. Have students find the correct word that matches each word part.
4. When the chart is completed, check against the Answer Key on page 21.
5. Then, have students pick a word from the chart and record it on their My Words chart.
6. Have students create a sentence for each word.
7. Have students read their sentences to their classmates.

## Suggestions

- Laminate cards for durability.
- Store each chart and set of cards in plastic zipper bags. Label the outside with the name of the chart.
- Use charts and cards in a center.

# My Words

**Name:** _____ **Date:**_____

**Directions:** Write the word and then make a sentence with the word.

**Word:** _____ **Sentence:** _____

_____

**Word:** _____ **Sentence:** _____

_____

**Word:** _____ **Sentence:** _____

_____

**Word:** _____ **Sentence:** _____

_____

**Word:** _____ **Sentence:** _____

_____

**Word:** _____ **Sentence:** _____

_____

# AI or AY?

 tr [ ] n

 d [ ]

 p [ ]

 pr [ ]

 gr [ ]

 r [ ] n

 sn [ ] l

 ch [ ] n

- - - - - - - - - - - - - - - - - - - - - - - - - - - - - - - - -

| ai | ai | ay | ay |
|----|----|----|----|
| ai | ai | ay | ay |

# AL, AU, or AW?

 ch [ ] k

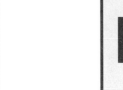 b [ ] l

 [ ] thor

 dr [ ]

 cr [ ] l

 [ ] tumn

 str [ ]

 w [ ] k

- - - - - - - - - - - - - - - - - - - - - - - - - -

| al | al | aw | aw |
|----|----|----|----|
| al | au | au | aw |

# EA or EE?

 tr [ ]

 wh [ ] t

 t [ ]

 thr [ ]

 sh [ ] p

 m [ ] t

 wh [ ] l

 l [ ] f

| ee | ee | ea | ea |
| ee | ee | ea | ea |

# ER, IR, or UR?

 riv☐

 sh☐t

 d☐t

 t☐tle

 n☐se

 bak☐

 g☐l

 p☐ple

- - - - - - - - - - - - - - - - - - - - - - - -

| ir | ir | ur | ur |
|----|----|----|----|
| ir | er | er | ur |

# OA or OW?

 b ⬜ t

 sn ⬜

 thr ⬜

 g ⬜ t

 s ⬜ p

 sh ⬜

 b ⬜ l

 r ⬜ d

- - - - - - - - - - - - - - - - - - - - - - - - - - -

| oa | oa | ow | ow |
|----|----|----|----|
| oa | oa | ow | ow |

# OI or Oy?

 ___ster

 p___nt

 b___

 c___n

 t___s

 b___l

 ___l

 j___

oi　　oi　　oy　　oy

oi　　oi　　oy　　oy

# OU or OW?

| ou | ou | ow | ow |
|----|----|----|----|
| ou | ou | ow | ow |

# Answer Key for "Same Sounds"

## AI or AY?

 tr<u>ai</u>n

 p<u>ay</u>

 gr<u>ay</u>

 sn<u>ai</u>l

 d<u>ay</u>

 pr<u>ay</u>

 r<u>ai</u>n

 ch<u>ai</u>n

## ER, IR, or UR?

 riv<u>er</u>

 d<u>ir</u>t

 n<u>ur</u>se

 g<u>ir</u>l

 sh<u>ir</u>t

 t<u>ur</u>tle

 bak<u>er</u>

 p<u>ur</u>ple

## OU or OW?

 fl<u>ow</u>er

 cr<u>ow</u>n

 cl<u>ow</u>n

 m<u>ou</u>th

 h<u>ou</u>se

 cl<u>ou</u>d

 br<u>ow</u>n

 m<u>ou</u>se

## AL, AU, or AW?

 ch<u>al</u>k

 <u>au</u>thor

 cr<u>aw</u>l

 str<u>aw</u>

 b<u>all</u>

 dr<u>aw</u>

 <u>au</u>tumn

 w<u>al</u>k

## OA or OW?

 b<u>oa</u>t

 thr<u>ow</u>

 s<u>oa</u>p

 b<u>ow</u>l

 sn<u>ow</u>

 g<u>oa</u>t

 sh<u>ow</u>

 r<u>oa</u>d

## EA or EE?

 tr<u>ee</u>

 t<u>ea</u>

 sh<u>ee</u>p

 wh<u>ee</u>l

 wh<u>ea</u>t

 thr<u>ee</u>

 m<u>ea</u>t

 l<u>ea</u>f

## OI or OY?

 <u>oy</u>ster

 b<u>oy</u>

 t<u>oy</u>s

 <u>oi</u>l

 p<u>oi</u>nt

 c<u>oi</u>n

 b<u>oi</u>l

 j<u>oy</u>

# Hooked on Meanings

## Skill

- Students identify word parts (prefixes, suffixes, Greek roots, and Latin roots) and their meanings.

## Grouping

- independent
- pairs
- small group

## Materials

- chart on page 25
- one of the following sets of word parts and their sample words:
  Prefixes (pages 27–33)
  Greek Roots (pages 35–37)
  Latin Roots (pages 39–41)
  Suffixes (pages 43–47)
- copies of My Meanings worksheet (page 24) for every student

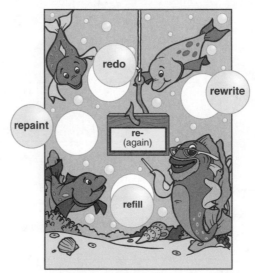

## Directions

1. Choose a set of word cards with which to work (prefixes, Greek roots, Latin roots, or suffixes).
2. Place the word parts [Example: *re–* (again)] in one pile and the word bubbles [Examples: *redo*, *repaint*, or *rewrite*] in another pile.
3. Have students choose a card containing a word part.
4. Have students read the word part and its meaning.
5. Have students place the word part card in the center of the chart.
6. Then, have students find the words (bubbles) that contain that word part.
7. Have them place the cards on the chart. (*Note*: There should be four words for every word part.)
8. Have students record the word part and its meaning on the My Meanings worksheet.
9. Have students choose one of the sample words that contains the word part.
10. Have students write a sentence containing the sample word and record it on the My Meanings worksheet. (*Note:* One example is done for you on the worksheet.)

## Suggestions

- Laminate chart and word cards.
- Have students create more words that contain the word parts. Then, make more blank cards (in the same size and shape of bubbles used in the activity) and have students write the words they created on the cards.
- As a challenge, have students alphabetize the word cards.

# My Meanings

**Name:** _____ **Date:**_____

**Directions:** Write the word part and its meaning. Then, make a sentence with a word that contains the word part. Study the example below. Use your dictionary to help you.

**Word Part:** _____re-_____ **Meaning:** _____again_____

**Sentence:** _____You will need to rewrite your paper._____

**Word Part:** _____ **Meaning:** _____

**Sentence:** _____

**Word Part:** _____ **Meaning:** _____

**Sentence:** _____

**Word Part:** _____ **Meaning:** _____

**Sentence:** _____

**Word Part:** _____ **Meaning:** _____

**Sentence:** _____

**Word Part:** _____ **Meaning:** _____

**Sentence:** _____

**incorrect**

**in-**
(not/opposite of)

**indirect**

**incomplete**

**inability**

**overdo**

**over-**
(too much)

**overripe**

**overcrowd**

**overeat**

**bicycle**

**bi-**
(two)

**bifocal**

**biweekly**

**biceps**

## dis-
### (not)

disagree

disloyal

dishonest

disarm

microphone

## micro-
### (small, short)

microbe

microscope

microfilm

misbehave

## mis-
### (bad)

misspell

mistake

miscount

**re-**
(again)

rewrite

redo

refill

repaint

**tele-**
(distant)

television

telephone

telegraph

telescope

**un-**
(not)

unhappy

unwrap

unable

unpaid

submarine

**sub-**
(under)

subsoil

subway

substation

prepay

**pre-**
(before)

prehistory

preschool

prearrange

nonfat

**non-**
(not)

nonstick

nonstop

nonsense

telegraph

**graph**
(write)

phonograph

photograph

autograph

thermometer

**meter**
(measure)

diameter

centimeter

barometer

**phon**
(sound)

phonograph

telephone

symphony

microphone

**bicycle**

**cycl**
(circle, ring)

**cycle**

**cyclone**

**cyclops**

**telegram**

**gram**
(letter, written)

**grammar**

**diagram**

**monogram**

**thermometer**

**therm**
(heat)

**thermostat**

**thermal**

**thermos**

**ang**
(bend)

angle

quadrangle

triangle

angular

**loc**
(place)

locate

relocate

dislocate

location

**ped**
(foot)

pedal

biped

pedestrian

pedestal

Teacher Created Resources

Teacher Created Resources

Teacher Created Resources

Teacher Created Resources

Teacher Created Resources

Teacher Created Resources

Teacher Created Resources

Teacher Created Resources

Teacher Created Resources

Teacher Created Resources

Teacher Created Resources

Teacher Created Resources

Teacher Created Resources

Teacher Created Resources

Teacher Created Resources

Teacher Created Resources

Teacher Created Resources

Teacher Created Resources

Teacher Created Resources

Teacher Created Resources

Teacher Created Resources

Teacher Created Resources

Teacher Created Resources

Teacher Created Resources

Teacher Created Resources

Teacher Created Resources

Teacher Created Resources

Teacher Created Resources

Teacher Created Resources

Teacher Created Resources

Teacher Created Resources

**port**
(carry)

transport

portable

import

porter

**rupt**
(break)

erupt

rupture

interrupt

bankrupt

**tract**
(pull, drag)

tractor

attraction

subtract

traction

daily

**-ly**
(every)

yearly

weekly

monthly

cameraman

**-man**
(one who works with)

doorman

salesman

mailman

fatter

**-er**
(more)

crazier

smarter

smaller

talked

**-ed, -d**
(past tense)

baked

walked

raised

teacher

**-er**
(one who)

seller

painter

shipper

pens

**-s, -es**
(plural)

books

boxes

foxes

prideful

**-ful**
(full of)

careful

joyful

helpful

careless

**-less**
(without)

thankless

seedless

useless

joyous

**-ous**
(full of)

nervous

famous

dangerous

# Story Puzzles

## Skill

- Students read a short story and identify either the homophone, synonym, or antonym.

## Grouping

- independent
- pairs
- small groups

## Materials

- one of the following stories and their matching cards:

  Homophone Story and Cards (pages 51–53)

  Synonym Story and Cards (pages 55–57)

  Antonym Story and Cards (pages 59–61)

- Answer Key (page 50)

## Directions

1. Choose one of the stories and cards with which to work (homophones, synonyms, or antonyms).

2. Explain to students what the focus will be in each story. For example, if you are having the students work on the synonym story, explain to students the meaning of a synonym and give some examples.

3. Have students read through the whole story.

4. Then, have students find the correct word cards to place on the white boxes.

5. After they have finished placing their cards on the story, have them read it through again, but now reading with the new word cards.

6. Have students use the Answer Key on page 50 to check their answers.

## Suggestions

- Laminate story puzzle sheets and word cards.
- Place the story puzzle sheets and word cards in a center.
- Have students create their own stories and cards. When the stories are complete, place students with partners. Have the partners read the stories.

# Answer Key

## Page 51 Homophone Story

Homophone Story                                        Story Puzzles

**Directions:** Read the story and match the pictures with the correct words.

The Tale of the **Bear**

**One** day there was a great big bear

who had lots of **hair**. He was walking

down the rocky **road** when he met a

**horse** and an **ant**. They smelled

a **flower** and played in the **sun**.

They played by the **creek**. The bear, the

horse, and the ant went home because it started

to **rain**.

## Page 55 Synonym Story

Synonym Story                                          Story Puzzles

**Directions:** Read the story and find the card that has the matching <u>synonym</u>.

The **Tiny** Bug

One **chilly** day a tiny bug heard a

**noisy** sound. He ran **quickly**.

The bug hid **below** a leaf. He felt very

**afraid** and **sad**. It started to

rain. The bug became very **damp**. The

sun came out and it was very **bright**.

The tiny bug dried off with a **grin** on

his face! "What a day!" he said.

## Page 59 Antonym Story

Antonym Story                                          Story Puzzles

**Directions:** Read the story and find the card that has the matching <u>antonym</u>.

The Ride

One **quiet** morning a **young**

man took a ride in a **small** car. The

car had a **full** tank of gas. He drove

it on a **dry** road. It was **hot**

so he reached to **open** the windows.

He stopped the car and a **kind** lady

gave him something cool to drink. He was so

**happy**! The drink tasted **sweet**

and it made the ride worth while!

**Directions:** Read the story and match the pictures with the correct words.

The Tale of the

 day there was a great big bear

who had lots of  . He was walking

down the rocky  when he met a

 and an  . They smelled

a  and played in the  .

They played by the  . The bear, the

horse, and the ant went home because it started

to  .

52

| Bear | Bare | One |
| :---: | :---: | :---: |
| hair | hare | Won |
| road | rode | horse |
| aunt | ant | hoarse |
| sun | son | flower |
| creek | creak | flour |
| rain | reign | |

**Directions:** Read the story and find the card that has the matching <u>synonym</u>.

The **Small** Bug

One **cold** day a tiny bug heard a

**loud** sound. He ran **fast** .

The bug hid **under** a leaf. He felt very

**scared** and **unhappy** . It started to

rain. The bug became very **wet** . The

sun came out and it was very **shiny** .

The tiny bug dried off with a **smile** on

his face! "What a day!" he said.

| | | |
|---|---|---|
| **Tiny** | **Large** | **chilly** |
| **noisy** | **quiet** | **hot** |
| **quickly** | **slowly** | **below** |
| **afraid** | **brave** | **over** |
| **damp** | **dry** | **sad** |
| **bright** | **dull** | **happy** |
| **grin** | **frown** | |

**Directions:** Read the story and find the card that has the matching <u>antonym</u>.

# The Ride

One **noisy** morning a **old**

man took a ride in a **big** car. The

car had a **empty** tank of gas. He drove

it on a **wet** road. It was **cold**

so he reached to **close** the windows.

He stopped the car and a **mean** lady

gave him something cool to drink. He was so

**sad** ! The drink tasted **sour**

and it made the ride worth while!

| quiet | loud | young |
|-------|------|-------|
| small | large | aged |
| full | unfilled | dry |
| hot | chilly | damp |
| open | shut | kind |
| happy | unhappy | unkind |
| sweet | bitter | |

# Story Starters

## Skill
- Students write stories using story starters.

## Grouping
- independent
- pairs
- small group
- whole group

## Materials
- Story Starter Strips (pages 65–75)
- Writing a Paragraph (page 64)
- pencils
- paper

## Directions
1. Write the following story starter on the board: "It was a very rainy day when _____."
2. Ask students to think of ideas to fill in the blank such as the following examples: "a car crashed into a tree," "I slipped and fell into a huge hole," or "my dad came home late."
3. Pick one idea and develop three or more supporting details for it. In the example of "a car crashed into a tree," you can use the following details: "First, the car was speeding down the highway. Next, the car hit a huge hole. Then it spun around and crashed into the tree."
4. With students, develop a concluding sentence such as the following: "It was a very bad car crash on that very rainy day."
5. Pass out the Writing a Paragraph page. Read it over with students so they understand the structure of their stories.
6. Tell students that they will get a story starter and will have to develop paragraphs for their stories.
7. Have students write their stories and check to see if any student needs support. Encourage them to ask their classmates for ideas to develop their stories.
8. When students are finished with writing their stories, have them read other classmates' stories and make any corrections or give suggestions.
9. Have students practice reading their final drafts of their stories. Encourage them to read their stories with fluency and expression. Have them read their stories to the class.

## Suggestions
- Laminate story starters for durability.
- Place the story starters in a writing center for students to use.
- Place all student stories in a book for students to read at a later time or for parents to read.

# Writing a Paragraph

**Topic Sentence:** It tells the reader what the paragraph is about.

Example: Trees give us many things.

**Supporting Sentences:** These are at least three details that expand the topic sentence. They help make the topic or main idea clearer and give more information about it.

Example: Trees give us shade on hot days.
Example: The wood on trees helps to build our homes.
Example: The leaves on the trees give oxygen to the air to help us breathe.

**Concluding Sentence:** The final sentence of a paragraph is the closing or concluding sentence. It comes at the end of the supporting details or the body of the paragraph. The concluding sentence should express the feeling, attitude, or point of the paragraph.

Example: What would we do without trees?

## TREES

Trees give us many things. Trees give us shade on hot days. The wood on trees helps to build our homes. The leaves on the trees give oxygen to the air to help us breathe. What would we do without trees?

The green door opened, and I saw _____.

I would like to know more about _____.

The biggest problem in the world is _____.

My favorite school subjects are _____.

I get really mad when _____.

If I were a cloud, I would _____.

The best TV show is _____.

If I were an ant, I would _____.

The best book I ever read was _____.

The amazing things I like to collect are _____.

My favorite place to be is _____.

The things I like to make are _____.

When I grow up, I will _____.

My favorite animal is _____.

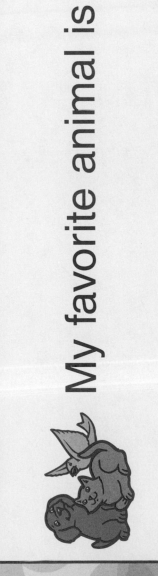

When nobody is around, I like to _____.

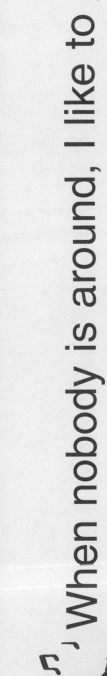

In school, the thing I like best is _____.

If I had a million dollars, I would _____.

Outside of school, the thing I like to do best is _____.

# Comprehension Cards

## Skill

- Students read a story and then answer questions about the story.

## Grouping

- independent
- pairs
- small group
- whole group

## Materials

- Comprehension Cards (Easy Second Grade on pages 79–84, Hard Second Grade on pages 85–90, Easy Third Grade on pages 91–96, and Hard Third Grade on pages 97–102)
- writing utensils and paper

## Directions

1. Choose one Comprehension Card with which to work. Make sure the level matches your students' abilities. You may wish to make multiple copies of the stories when working with a whole group. You also can enlarge the comprehension card to a poster size and then read the story together.
2. Read the story on the card. Encourage fluency and expression. Students may wish to reread the story again or read the story aloud with a partner.
3. Answer the questions below the story.
4. Have students record their answers on paper.
5. Have students check their answers with the Answer Key on the back of each card.

## Suggestions

- Laminate cards for durability.
- Give each student a copy of the story. Have him or her find the important details in the story. For example, you could have the students circle the main characters or draw a square around the setting. Have them highlight important or unfamiliar vocabulary words.
- Enlarge each card to a poster size and post them on a wall. Encourage students to read the stories as they walk by them.
- Use the comprehension cards in a reading and writing center.
- Have students write more questions to the story they read. Have their partners answer their questions.
- Have students use the blank card on page 78 to create more comprehension cards. Have them write stories and develop questions and answers to their stories. Have students write drafts first and then write their final stories and questions on the blank card. You also can have each student type his or her story on the computer, print it out, and then glue the typed story onto the blank card.

# Playing in the Snow

I have fun in the snow. First, I have snowball fights. Then, I build a snowman. Next, I ride down the hill on my sled. The snow is so much fun!

## Questions

1. What is the main idea?
   - a. how to build a snowman
   - b. how to sled
   - c. how to ski
   - d. playing in the snow

2. What is the topic sentence?
   - a. The snow is so much fun!
   - b. Then, I build a snowman.
   - c. I have fun in the snow.
   - d. First, I have snowball fights.

3. What did the author build from snow?
   - a. a sled
   - b. a snowman
   - c. a fence
   - d. a hill

4. What season might this story take place?
   - a. winter
   - b. spring
   - c. fall
   - d. summer

# Answers

**1.** d.

**2.** c.

**3.** b.

**4.** a.

# Rainy Days

I like to do three things on rainy days. The first thing I like to do on rainy days is bake cookies. Next, I like to write letters to my grandmothers. After baking and writing, I like to read. When I do these three things, I like rainy days.

**Questions**

1. What kind of weather does the author talk about?
   - a. hot
   - b. warm
   - c. snowy
   - d. rainy

2. How many things does the author like to do on rainy days?
   - a. one
   - b. two
   - c. three
   - d. four

3. What is the first thing the author likes to do on rainy days?
   - a. write letters
   - b. bake cookies
   - c. read a book
   - d. step in water puddles

4. Do you think the author likes rainy days?
   - a. No
   - b. Yes
   - c. Maybe
   - d. Doesn't say

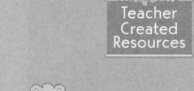

# Answers

**1.** d.

**2.** c.

**3.** b.

**4.** b.

# Fishing Is Fun

Fishing is fun for many reasons. It is fun to be out in a boat on a lake or along a stream in the woods. The most exciting part of fishing is catching a fish. Until I actually have the fish in the net, I am not sure that I am going to able to keep it on the hook. One of the best parts of fishing is eating the fish that has been cooked on an open fire. It is hard to beat fishing when it comes to having a good time!

## Questions

1. What is the story about?
   - a. boating
   - b. cooking
   - c. fishing
   - d. eating

2. What does the author think is the <u>most</u> exciting part about fishing?
   - a. looking at a fish
   - b. catching a fish
   - c. swimming with a fish
   - d. riding in a boat

3. Which title could go with this story?
   - a. In the Woods
   - b. Being on a Boat
   - c. How to Cook a Fish
   - d. Why I Like to Fish

4. Do you think the writer likes to fish?
   - a. No
   - b. Yes
   - c. Sometimes
   - d. It doesn't say

# Answers

**1.** c.

**2.** b.

**3.** d.

**4.** b.

# My Older Sister

My older sister really bothers me. She gets into my things. She was in my room again yesterday. She thinks she always has to check on me even if there is an adult in the house. She even asks me questions about my friends. She also asks me how I am doing in school. She wants to know if I get along with my teacher. She probably thinks I should ask permission before I go anywhere or do anything. She is the most annoying older sister you could ever imagine. She should not try to run my life!

## Questions

1. Who is this passage about?
   - a. older brother
   - b. teacher
   - c. older sister
   - d. mother

2. Where does this passage take place?
   - a. at a house
   - b. at the mall
   - c. at school
   - d. at a restaurant

3. The older sister asks questions about everything <u>except</u>
   - a. friends
   - b. school
   - c. teacher
   - d. clothes

4. How do you think the author feels about his or her older sister?
   - a. hateful
   - b. annoyed
   - c. lovable
   - d. doesn't say

# Answers

**1.** c.
**2.** a.
**3.** d.
**4.** b.

# A Night at the Circus

I love to go to the circus. On May 6, the circus came to my hometown of Jackson, Wyoming. A parade marched through our streets and soon the big top could be seen. Ken and I went to watch the performers prepare for opening night. We saw clowns, acrobats, and even the ringmaster. What a sight! You should go if you ever get the chance to spend a night at the circus.

## Questions

1. What day did the circus come to Jackson, Wyoming?
   - a. May 6
   - b. May 8
   - c. May 4
   - d. May 16

2. The author watched the performance with whom?
   - a. Jackson
   - b. May
   - c. Ken
   - d. Alice

3. At the circus, the author saw everything except
   - a. clowns.
   - b. donkeys.
   - c. acrobats.
   - d. the ringmaster.

4. What animals might the author have seen at the circus?
   - a. horses
   - b. bats
   - c. wolves
   - d. crocodiles

# Answers

**1.** a.
**2.** c.
**3.** b.
**4.** a.

# Cory's Garden

It was a sunny day, and Cory was digging in his garden. He had a special box just for tomatoes and carrots, but right now he was watering his sunflowers. They were very tall, taller than Cory. Each sunflower had bright yellow petals. The sunflowers grew straight to the sky, except one. One sunflower leaned over the fence as if to talk to Cory's dog, Sid.

Sid barked at the sunflower, but the sunflower didn't answer. Sid barked again and then sat down. Cory put down his watering can and opened the gate.

"Okay, Sid," he said, "The flower won't talk to you, but I will. Time to play!"

Sid wagged his tail with happiness.

## Questions

1. How was the weather when Cory was working in his garden?
   a. rainy
   b. cold
   c. windy
   d. sunny

2. What items were <u>not</u> mentioned in the story?
   a. tomatoes
   b. carrots
   c. roses
   d. sunflowers

3. Why was Cory's dog, Sid, barking?
   a. Cory didn't open the gate.
   b. He wanted some water.
   c. The sunflower didn't talk to him.
   d. He was hungry.

4. To grow a garden, you need everything <u>except</u>
   a. a hammer.
   b. sunlight.
   c. soil.
   d. water.

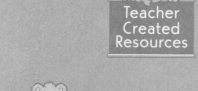

# Answers

**1.** d.

**2.** c.

**3.** c.

**4.** a.

# Farmer Gray's Morning

Farmer Gray woke up as the sun was rising. He had a lot of work to do. He went outside and looked at the sky. A storm was <u>brewing</u> in the distance. He knew he needed to hurry. So he went to the barn and gave fresh hay to the horses. He cleaned the pigpen and fed the chickens. He checked the hen house and collected the eggs from the nests. He ran inside and put the eggs in the refrigerator. Then, he hiked out to the pasture to check on the cows. As Farmer Gray headed back to the house, the sky grew dark and it started to rain. He made it to the house as the storm showered down on him. He opened the door and smelled eggs and bacon cooking in the kitchen. All that work, and the day had only just begun!

### Questions

**1.** What does the word <u>brewing</u> mean in the third line?
    a. boiling          c. shining
    b. forming        d. digging

**2.** How would you describe Farmer Gray's morning?
    a. lazy            c. busy
    b. relaxing       d. dull

**3.** Who do you think might have cooked the bacon and eggs?
    a. a baby         c. the mail person
    b. his wife        d. a dog

**4.** You would probably <u>not</u> find which animal on a farm?
    a. zebra          c. sheep
    b. chicken       d. pig

# Answers

**1.** b.

**2.** c.

**3.** b.

**4.** a.

# Molly's First Pet

Molly was so excited that she practically danced into the pet shop.  She was about to meet her first pet!  Her mother had promised her that she could choose a small animal.  Molly looked at bunnies, hamsters, rats, and mice.  There were so many to choose from!  She wondered how she could decide.

Then, in the corner cage, she saw the cutest animal she'd ever seen.  With its black and white bands of fur, it looked like a tiny panda bear.  Molly knew that she wanted that guinea pig.

### Questions

**1.** How did Molly feel about her first pet?
   a. excited
   b. sad
   c. mad
   d. scared

**2.** What pet did Molly decide on?
   a. a bunny
   b. a panda bear
   c. a hamster
   d. a guinea pig

**3.** To what did Molly compare her guinea pig?
   a. a rat
   b. a panda bear
   c. a dog
   d. a kitten

**4.** To live, a pet needs everything <u>except</u>
   a. water.
   b. food.
   c. shelter.
   d. toys.

# Answers

**1.** a.

**2.** d.

**3.** b.

**4.** d.

# The Last Match

The deep shadows of the forest seemed to press closer as if wrapping Ron in a cloak. He wished he could get a fire started. Something had gone wrong with each match he had lit. His shaking hands had dropped the first one. The second fizzled out on leaves that weren't dry enough to catch fire. The third he'd held to the <u>kindling</u> until it burned his fingertips. Ron had only one more match. If he failed to get a fire going with this one, he'd spend the night in this heavy darkness.

## Questions

1. Where does this story take place?
   - a. on a beach
   - b. in a forest
   - c. in a desert
   - d. in a jungle

2. How many matches did Ron have altogether?
   - a. three
   - b. four
   - c. five
   - d. six

3. What do you think the word <u>kindling</u> might mean?
   - a. rocks
   - b. dirt
   - c. sticks and wood
   - d. metal

4. How do you think Ron would feel if he failed to get the fire lit?
   - a. excited
   - b. jealous
   - c. bored
   - d. scared

# Answers

**1.** b.

**2.** b.

**3.** c.

**4.** d.

# Georgie the Giraffe

Although Georgie the giraffe was just a baby, he was taller than any of the adults in his herd. In fact, he was the only one who could reach to the very top of the tallest tree in the area. Georgie felt so proud of himself that he bragged and showed off for the other giraffes whenever he got the chance.

One day the herd of giraffes wandered to a new area. They came to a huge tree, taller than any other they had ever seen. Georgie wanted to show off. So he said, " Look at me! I can eat the leaves from the very top of this tall tree." With that he poked his head high up into the limbs of the gigantic tree. With a loud crack, several branches broke. They fell around his head, pinning down his ears. Georgie struggled, but the branches held him firmly. He cried to the rest of the giraffes, "Help me! My head is caught in the branches. I can't get loose!"

## Questions

**1.** What was so special about Georgie the Giraffe?
- a. He was the youngest giraffe.
- b. He could eat the most leaves.
- c. He could break branches.
- d. He could reach the tallest tree.

**2.** What problem did Georgie have?
- a. He didn't have any friends.
- b. His head was caught in the tree.
- c. He couldn't find any leaves to eat.
- d. He was too short to reach the tree.

**3.** How would you describe Georgie?
- a. shy
- b. proud
- c. smart
- d. thankful

**4.** What lesson do you think Georgie learned?
- a. Don't show off.
- b. Don't eat big leaves.
- c. Don't wander from the herd.
- d. Don't break branches.

# Answers

**1.** d.

**2.** b.

**3.** b.

**4.** a.

# Hiding Place

Just then the boys heard the sound of keys jingling as someone approached the door of the room. The boys looked wildly at each other, certain that any second they would hear the sound of the key in the lock.

"Hide!" Dan whispered, urgently pointing toward the crates.

The boys hurried behind the boxes stacked in one corner of the room. Over the top of the crates someone had thrown a rug. It draped down over both edges of the stack. With any luck, it would help to conceal them completely. No sooner had they hidden themselves than they heard the door open. They froze in position, determined not to move a muscle. Tom fought the urge to sneeze.

A light switch clicked on and light filled the room. Footsteps came toward the crates. Both boys held their breath. Had the person heard them?

## Questions

1. What part did the keys play in the story?
   a. They were lost.
   b. They did not fit.
   c. They made noise.
   d. They dropped on the floor.

2. The boys were hiding
   a. in a box.
   b. in the next room.
   c. in a corner.
   d. behind the door.

3. You would judge that the boys were
   a. scared.
   b. relieved.
   c. unhappy.
   d. starting to run.

4. When did this story happen?
   a. in the morning
   b. at night
   c. after school
   d. during a storm

# Answers

**1.** c.

**2.** c.

**3.** a.

**4.** b.

# Monkey's Trick

"Break the cage latch with your paws or your teeth," the monkey <u>advised</u>.

The lion tried and tried, but he just couldn't free the monkey. The latch wouldn't budge. Suddenly, the animals saw the plane's cargo hatch closing. The door slammed, leaving them trapped.

Now the lion was angry and hungry. He roared, "You tricked me!"

"I did not! I had no idea the door would close!" The monkey shouted over the roar of the engines. The plane shook from the noise.

The plane started to move—slowly at first, then faster and faster. The front of the plane lifted into the air, making the lion fall against the monkey's cage with such force that the latch broke open. After a few moments, both animals could move around.

"Where is the food you promised me?" the lion demanded. "Show it to me, or I'll eat you!"

"Look here," said the monkey, hopping over to a stack of large bags. "Eat all you like."

"You lured me here to eat dry cat food? I should eat you right now!" snarled the lion.

## Questions

1. What does the word <u>advised</u> mean in the first line?
   a. suggested
   b. yelled
   c. called
   d. whispered

2. What did the monkey promise the lion?
   a. a vacation
   b. food
   c. a nice seat on the plane
   d. a cage with a latch

3. What was the monkey's trick?
   a. He opened the cage himself.
   b. He closed the hatch.
   c. The food was cat food.
   d. He disappeared in the cage.

4. What word would describe the mood of the lion?
   a. happy
   b. upset
   c. sad
   d. thankful

# Answers

**1.** a.

**2.** b.

**3.** c.

**4.** b.

# Instant Words Activity Boards

## Skill

- Students read Instant Words (151–300)

## Grouping

- pairs
- small group
- whole class

## Materials

- Instant Words Activity Board (pages 106–107, 110–111, 114–115, 118–119, 122–123, or 126–127)
- game marker for each student (coins, colored paper clips, etc.)
- die

## Directions

1. Choose one of the following activity boards that suits the needs of your students:

   Instant Words Activity Board (151–175) on pages 106–107
   Instant Words Activity Board (176–200) on pages 110–111
   Instant Words Activity Board (201–225) on pages 114–115
   Instant Words Activity Board (226–250) on pages 118–119
   Instant Words Activity Board (251–275) on pages 122–123
   Instant Words Activity Board (276–300) on pages 126–127

2. Place the activity board on a flat surface with a die.
3. Have students place their markers on the starting area of the board.
4. Have each student take a turn by rolling the die.
5. Have students move their markers the number shown on the die.
6. When students move their markers, have them read the word on the space they landed. If a student reads the word correctly, he or she may keep his or her marker on that space. If a student does not read the word correctly, the turn is lost. (*Note:* You may leave the option open for the student to ask another student for help.)

## Suggestions

- Have students make flashcards of the words they need to learn. Have students take the flashcards home for practice.
- Use the assessment record on page 104 to keep track of which students have successfully read the words on each activity board.
- Have students add the words on the activity board to their personal dictionaries.
- Use the activity boards for centers or send them home for students to practice.

# Assessment Record

**NAME OF STUDENT**

| | Instant Words Activity Board (151–175) | Instant Words Activity Board (176–200) | Instant Words Activity Board (201–225) | Instant Words Activity Board (226–250) | Instant Words Activity Board (251–275) | Instant Words Activity Board (276–300) |
|---|---|---|---|---|---|---|
| | | | | | | |
| | | | | | | |
| | | | | | | |
| | | | | | | |
| | | | | | | |
| | | | | | | |
| | | | | | | |
| | | | | | | |
| | | | | | | |
| | | | | | | |
| | | | | | | |
| | | | | | | |
| | | | | | | |
| | | | | | | |
| | | | | | | |
| | | | | | | |
| | | | | | | |
| | | | | | | |
| | | | | | | |

Teacher Created Resources

Teacher Created Resources

Teacher Created Resources

Teacher Created Resources

Teacher Created Resources

Teacher Created Resources

Teacher Created Resources

Teacher Created Resources

Teacher Created Resources

Teacher Created Resources

Teacher Created Resources

Teacher Created Resources

Teacher Created Resources

Teacher Created Resources

Teacher Created Resources

Teacher Created Resources

Teacher Created Resources

Teacher Created Resources

Teacher Created Resources

Teacher Created Resources

Teacher Created Resources

Teacher Created Resources

Teacher Created Resources

Teacher Created Resources

Teacher Created Resources

Teacher Created Resources

Teacher Created Resources

Teacher Created Resources

Teacher Created Resources

Teacher Created Resources

Teacher Created Resources

Teacher Created Resources

Teacher Created Resources

Teacher Created Resources

Teacher Created Resources

Teacher Created Resources

Teacher Created Resources

Teacher Created Resources

Teacher Created Resources

Teacher Created Resources

Teacher Created Resources

Teacher Created Resources

Teacher Created Resources

Teacher Created Resources

Teacher Created Resources

Teacher Created Resources

Teacher Created Resources

Teacher Created Resources

Teacher Created Resources

Teacher Created Resources

Teacher Created Resources

Teacher Created Resources

Teacher Created Resources

Teacher Created Resources

Teacher Created Resources

Teacher Created Resources

Teacher Created Resources

Teacher Created Resources

Teacher Created Resources

Teacher Created Resources

Teacher Created Resources

Teacher Created Resources

Teacher Created Resources

Teacher Created Resources

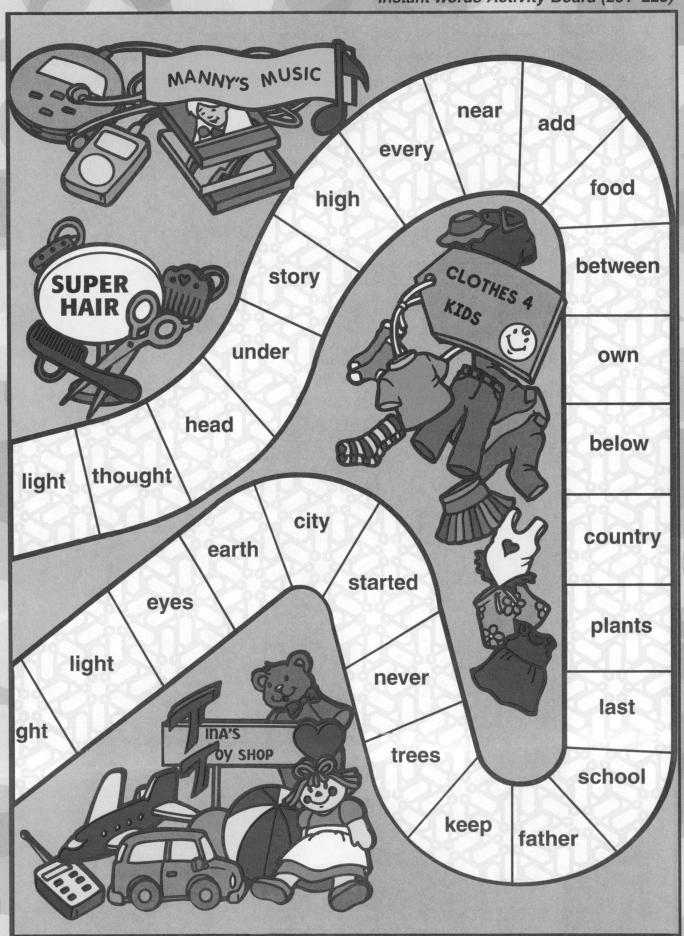

Teacher Created Resources
Teacher Created Resources
Teacher Created Resources
Teacher Created Resources

Teacher Created Resources
Teacher Created Resources
Teacher Created Resources

Teacher Created Resources
Teacher Created Resources
Teacher Created Resources
Teacher Created Resources

Teacher Created Resources
Teacher Created Resources
Teacher Created Resources

Teacher Created Resources
Teacher Created Resources
Teacher Created Resources
Teacher Created Resources

Teacher Created Resources
Teacher Created Resources
Teacher Created Resources

Teacher Created Resources
Teacher Created Resources
Teacher Created Resources
Teacher Created Resources

Teacher Created Resources
Teacher Created Resources
Teacher Created Resources

Teacher Created Resources
Teacher Created Resources
Teacher Created Resources
Teacher Created Resources

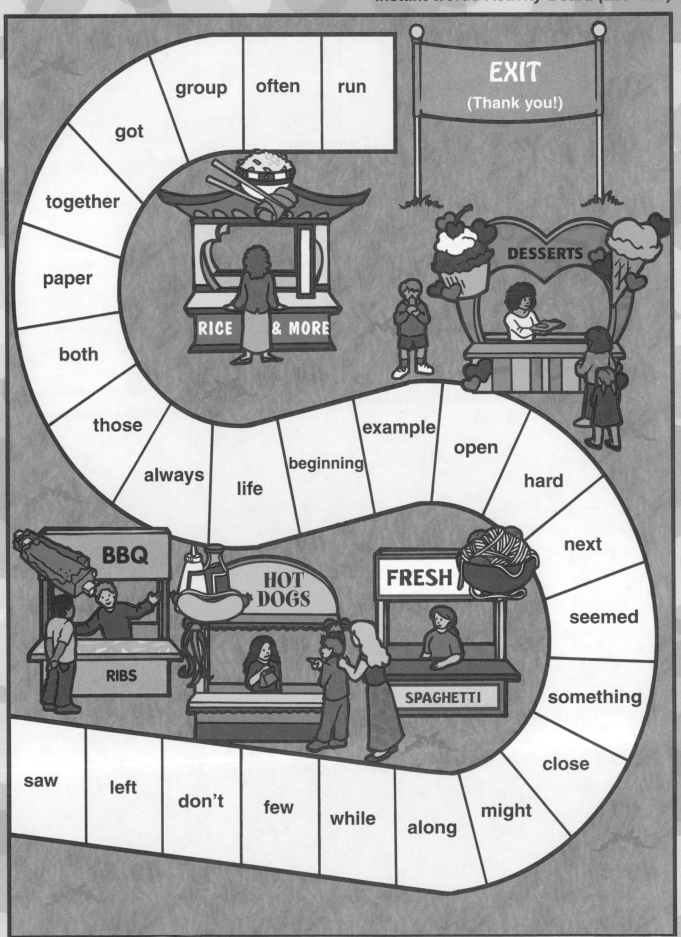

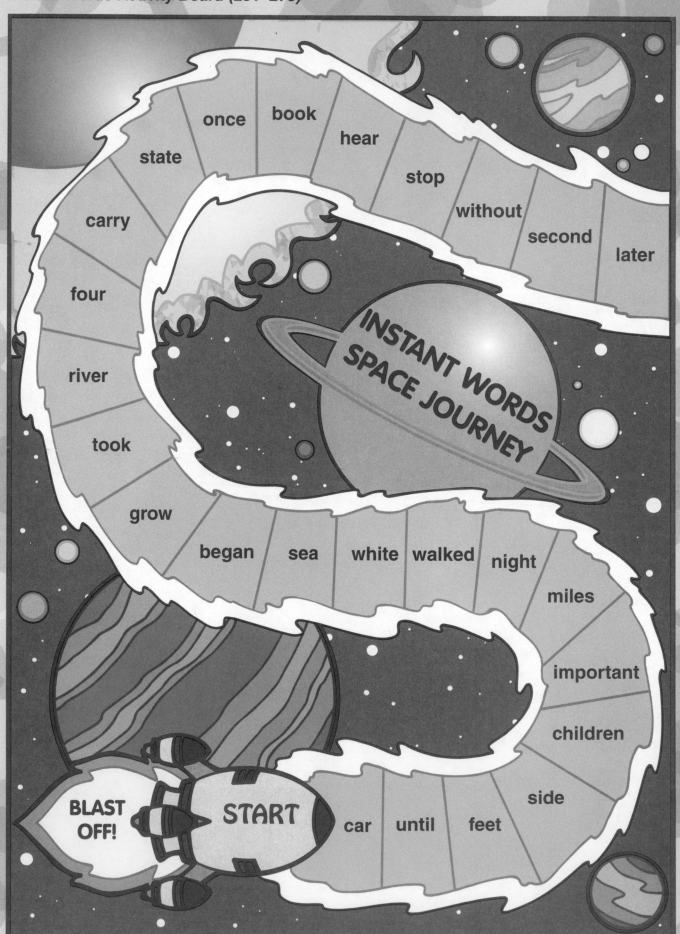

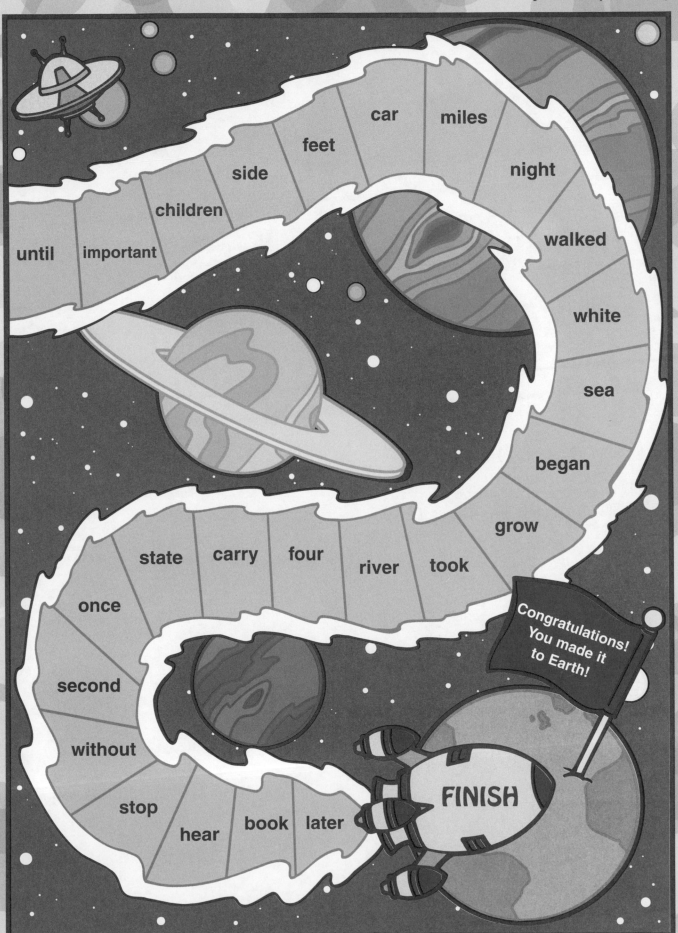

Teacher Created Resources

Teacher Created Resources

Teacher Created Resources

Teacher Created Resources

Teacher Created Resources

Teacher Created Resources

Teacher Created Resources

Teacher Created Resources

Teacher Created Resources

Teacher Created Resources

Teacher Created Resources

Teacher Created Resources

Teacher Created Resources

Teacher Created Resources

Teacher Created Resources

Teacher Created Resources

Teacher Created Resources

Teacher Created Resources

Teacher Created Resources

Teacher Created Resources

Teacher Created Resources

Teacher Created Resources

Teacher Created Resources

Teacher Created Resources

Teacher Created Resources

Teacher Created Resources

Teacher Created Resources

Teacher Created Resources

Teacher Created Resources

Teacher Created Resources

Teacher Created Resources

Teacher Created Resources

INSTANT WORDS
JUNGLE ADVENTURE

Beware of Danger!

START

miss idea eat face enough watch far Indians really almost let above girl sometimes mountains cut young talk soon list song being leave family it's

YOU SURVIVED!
Come Back Again!

being
leave
family
it's
song
list
soon
talk
young
cut
let
above
girl
sometimes
mountains
almost
really
Indians
far
watch
enough
face
eat
idea
miss

# Perfect Pairs

## Skill
- Students learn to read Instant Words (151–300)

## Grouping
- two to five people

## Materials
- one deck of same-colored Perfect Pairs cards

  Instant Words 151–175 deck (pages 131–137)    Instant Words 226–250 deck (pages 149–155)

  Instant Words 176–200 deck (pages 137–143)    Instant Words 251–275 deck (pages 155–161)

  Instant Words 201–225 deck (pages 143–149)    Instant Words 276–300 deck (pages 161–167)

## Directions
1. Have a student deal five cards to each player and place the remainder of the deck in the center of the table.
2. Tell students that the object of the game is to get as many pairs as possible. Tell them that there are only two cards alike in each deck.
3. The player to the right of the dealer may ask any other player for a specific card. For example, "Do you have *took*?" The player asking must have the mate (in the example, the *took* card) in his or her hand. The player who is asked must give up the card if he or she has it. If the first player does not get the card asked for, he or she draws one card from the pile. Then, the next player has a turn asking for a card.
4. If the player succeeds in getting the card asked for, either from another player or from the pile, he or she gets another turn. If the player gets a pair, it is placed down in front of him or her. The player with the most pairs at the end of the game wins. If the player doing the asking does not know how to read the word on the card, he or she may show the card and ask any of the other players or anyone present. If the player who is asked for a card does not know how to read that word or unsure of himself or herself, the best thing to do is ask to see the card of the other player requesting the card or ask a non-playing person who can read to look at his or her hand. (*Note:* A few extra blank cards are provided on page 167 to make color copies for adding more words.)

## Suggestions
- Match the decks to the level of the students. Students should know some but not all of the words used in a particular deck. They should have help in playing until they know almost all the words and can get along by themselves. They should play the game on several different occasions until they can call out all the words instantly. For beginning readers, create a custom deck or shorten the deck.
- Have students record their pairs on the recording sheet on page 130.
- Lay the cards face down on a flat surface. Use the cards to play a game of Memory. Each player turns over two cards. If they are a pair, he or she keeps them. If they are not a pair, then the cards must be put back in exactly the same place, face down. Students must remember the location of cards so they can make a pair. The students must read aloud each card turned over. If he or she doesn't know how to read the card, another player can read the word aloud.

# Perfect Pairs Recording Sheet

**Name:** _____ **Date:** _____

**Directions:** Record each word pair on the lines below.

**Word Pair 1:** _____ _____

**Word Pair 2:** _____ _____

**Word Pair 3:** _____ _____

**Word Pair 4:** _____ _____

**Word Pair 5:** _____ _____

**Word Pair 6:** _____ _____

**Word Pair 7:** _____ _____

**Word Pair 8:** _____ _____

**Word Pair 9:** _____ _____

**Word Pair 10:** _____ _____

**Word Pair 11:** _____ _____

**Word Pair 12:** _____ _____

**Word Pair 13:** _____ _____

**Word Pair 14:** _____ _____

**Word Pair 15:** _____ _____

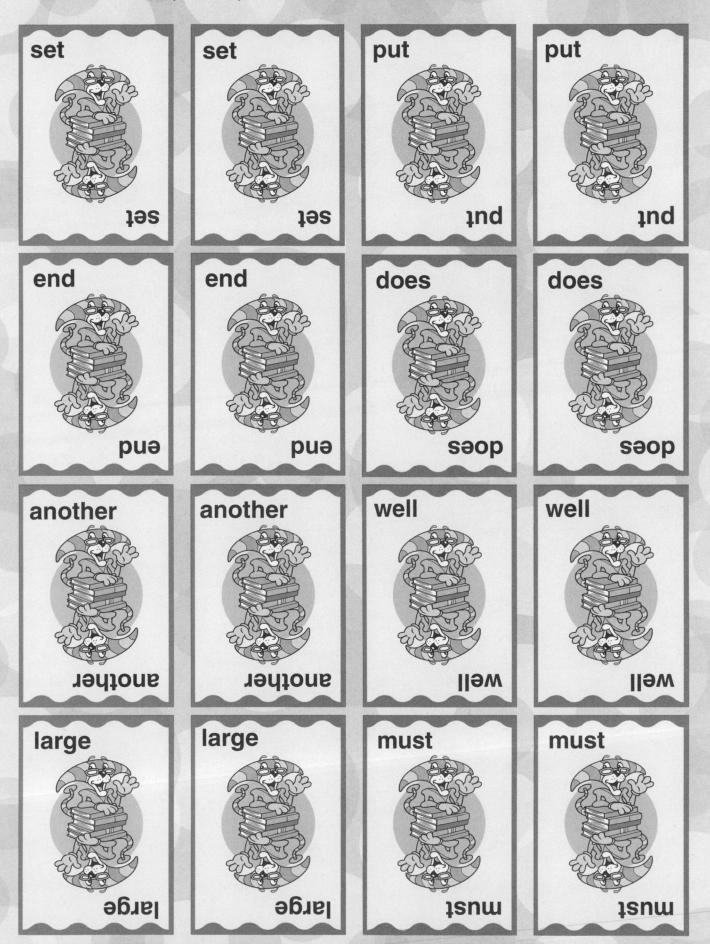

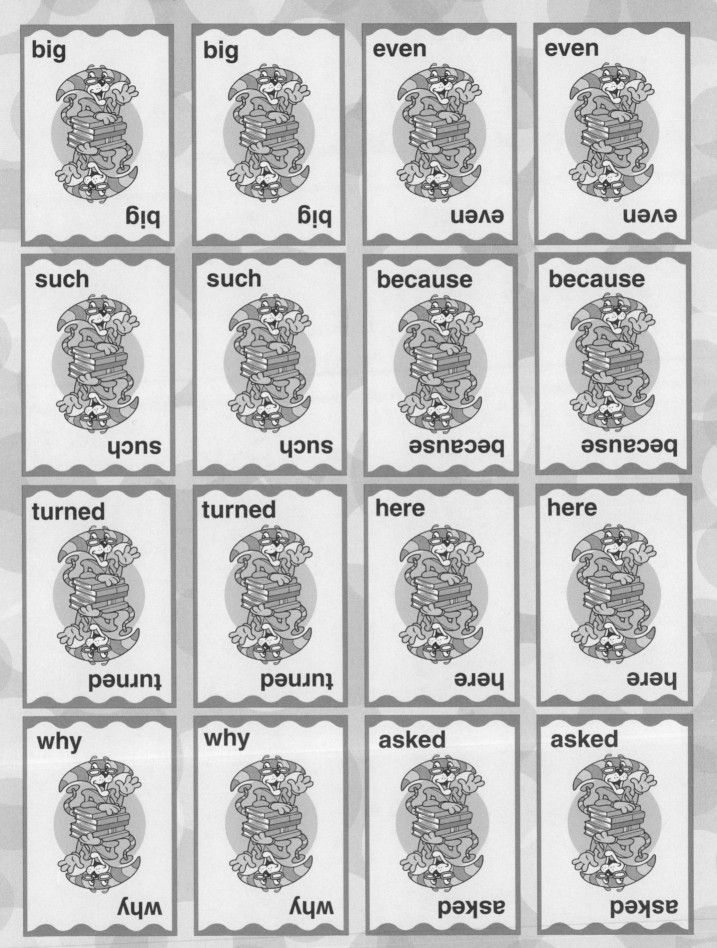

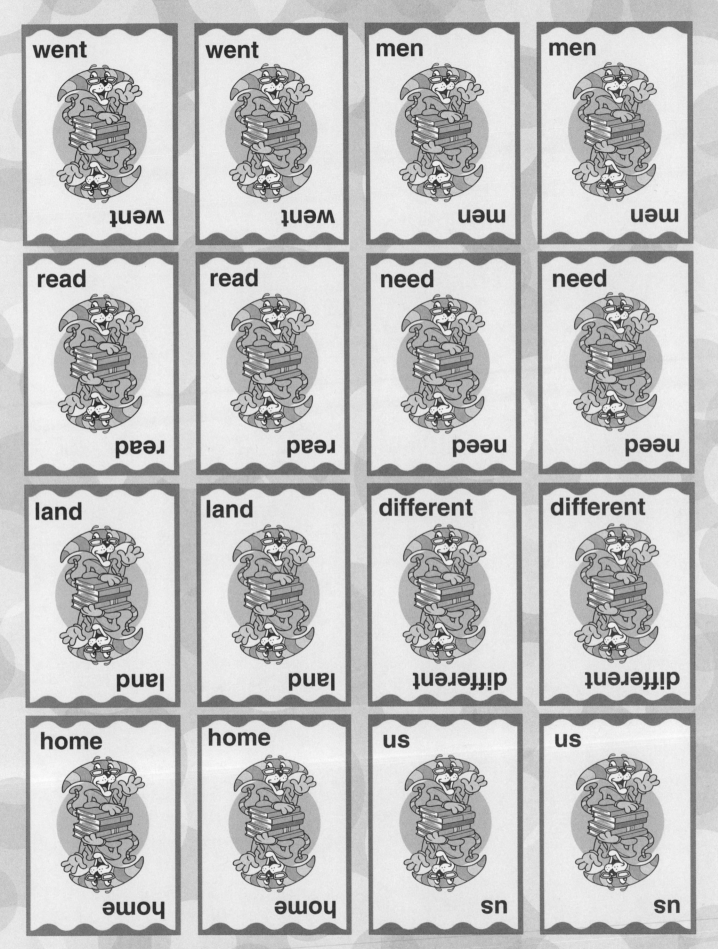

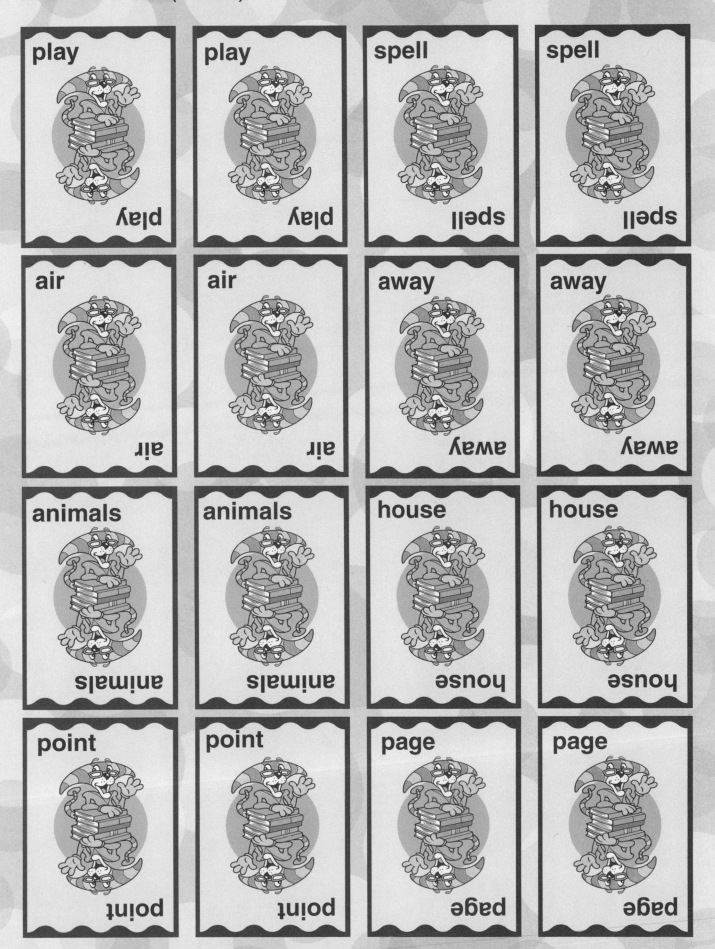

Teacher Created Resources

Teacher Created Resources

Teacher Created Resources

Teacher Created Resources

Teacher Created Resources

Teacher Created Resources

Teacher Created Resources

Teacher Created Resources

Teacher Created Resources

Teacher Created Resources

Teacher Created Resources

Teacher Created Resources

Teacher Created Resources

Teacher Created Resources

Teacher Created Resources

Teacher Created Resources

Teacher Created Resources

Teacher Created Resources

Teacher Created Resources

Teacher Created Resources

Teacher Created Resources

Teacher Created Resources

Teacher Created Resources

Teacher Created Resources

Teacher Created Resources

Teacher Created Resources

Teacher Created Resources

Teacher Created Resources

Teacher Created Resources

Teacher Created Resources

Teacher Created Resources

Teacher Created Resources

**American**

American

**American**

American

**world**

world

**world**

world

**high**

high

**high**

high

**every**

every

**every**

every

**near**

near

**near**

near

**add**

add

**add**

add

**food**

food

**food**

food

**between**

between

**between**

between

**own**

**own**

**below**

**below**

**country**

**country**

**plants**

**plants**

**last**

**last**

**school**

**school**

**father**

**father**

**keep**

**keep**

trees

trees

trees

trees

never

never

never

never

started

started

started

started

city

city

city

city

earth

earth

earth

earth

eyes

eyes

eyes

eyes

light

light

light

light

thought

thought

thought

thought

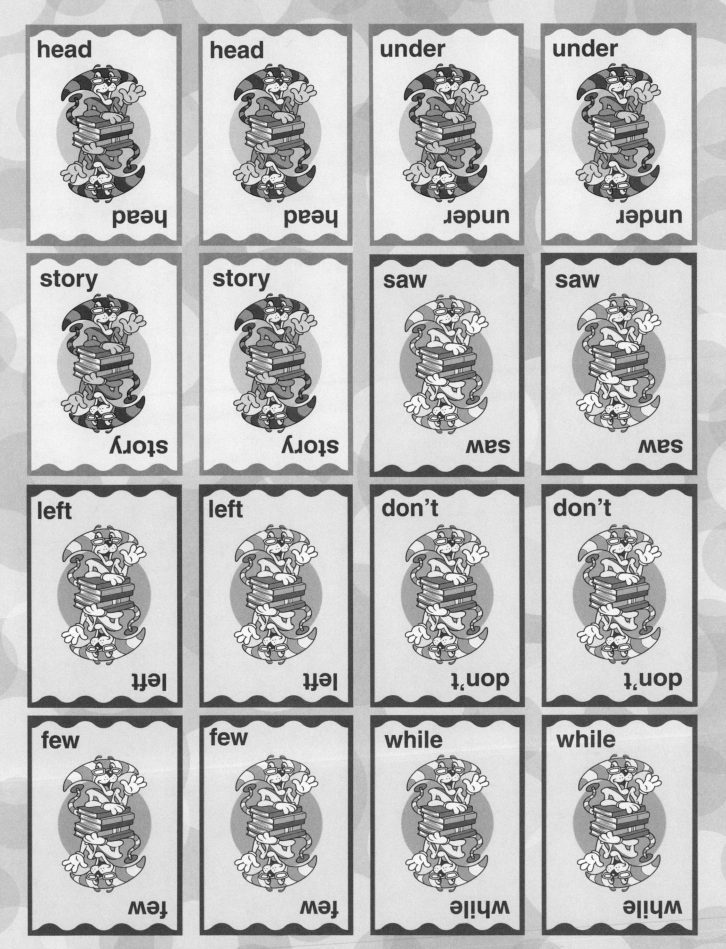

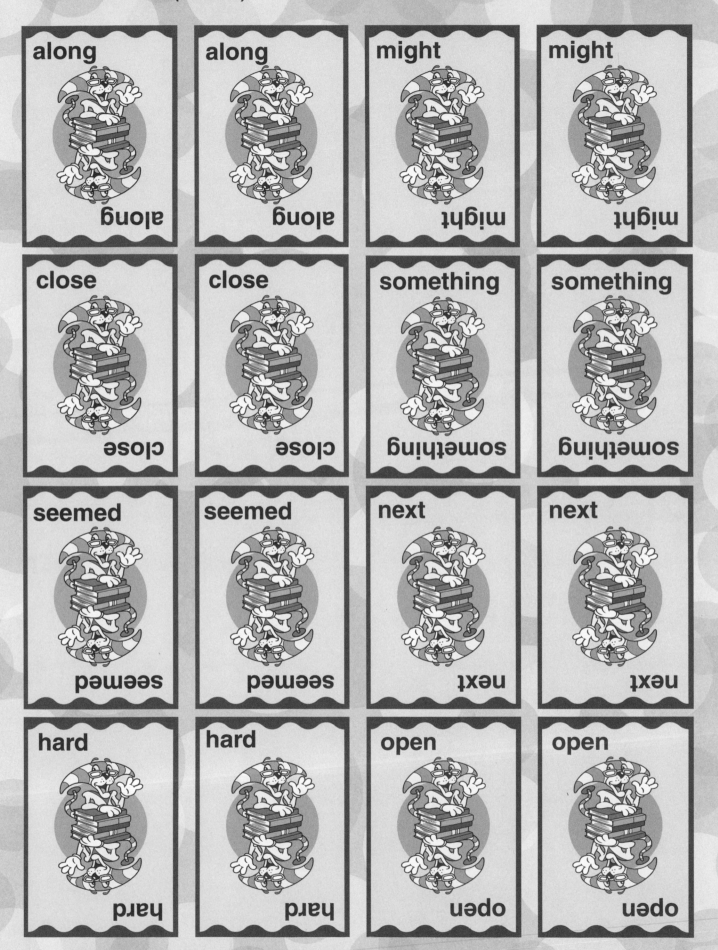

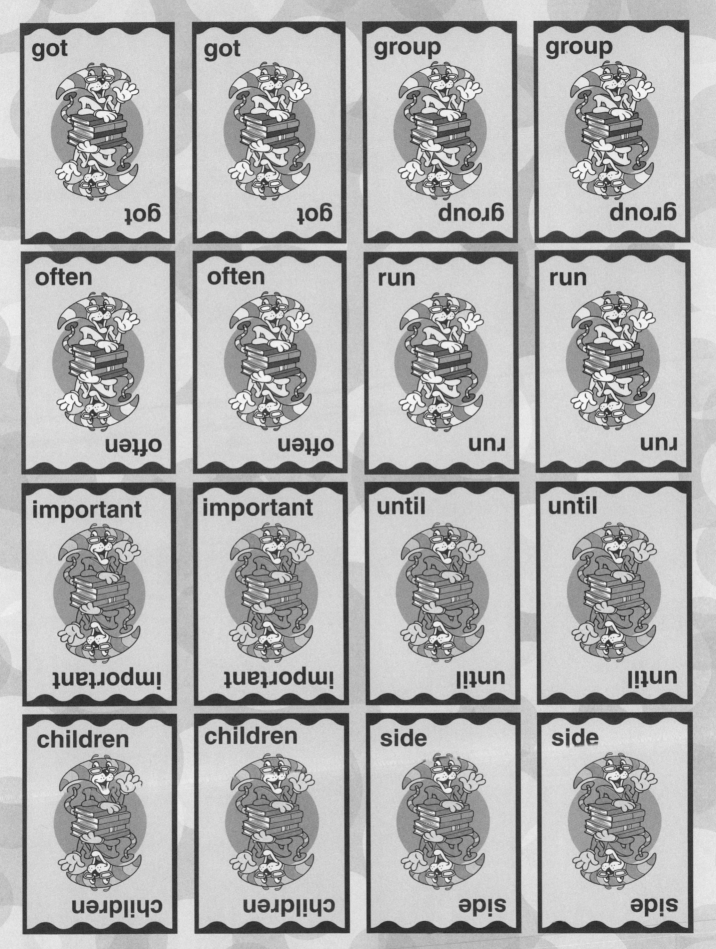

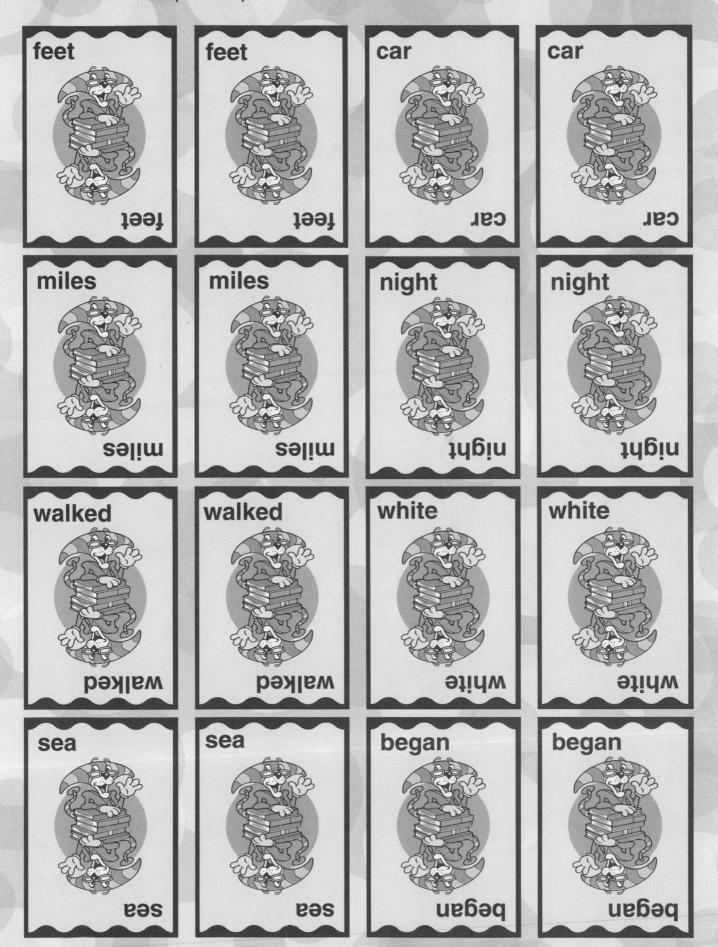

Teacher Created Resources

Teacher Created Resources

Teacher Created Resources

Teacher Created Resources

Teacher Created Resources

Teacher Created Resources

Teacher Created Resources

Teacher Created Resources

Teacher Created Resources

Teacher Created Resources

Teacher Created Resources

Teacher Created Resources

Teacher Created Resources

Teacher Created Resources

Teacher Created Resources

Teacher Created Resources

Teacher Created Resources

Teacher Created Resources

Teacher Created Resources

Teacher Created Resources

Teacher Created Resources

Teacher Created Resources

Teacher Created Resources

Teacher Created Resources

Teacher Created Resources

Teacher Created Resources

Teacher Created Resources

Teacher Created Resources

Teacher Created Resources

Teacher Created Resources

Teacher Created Resources

Teacher Created Resources

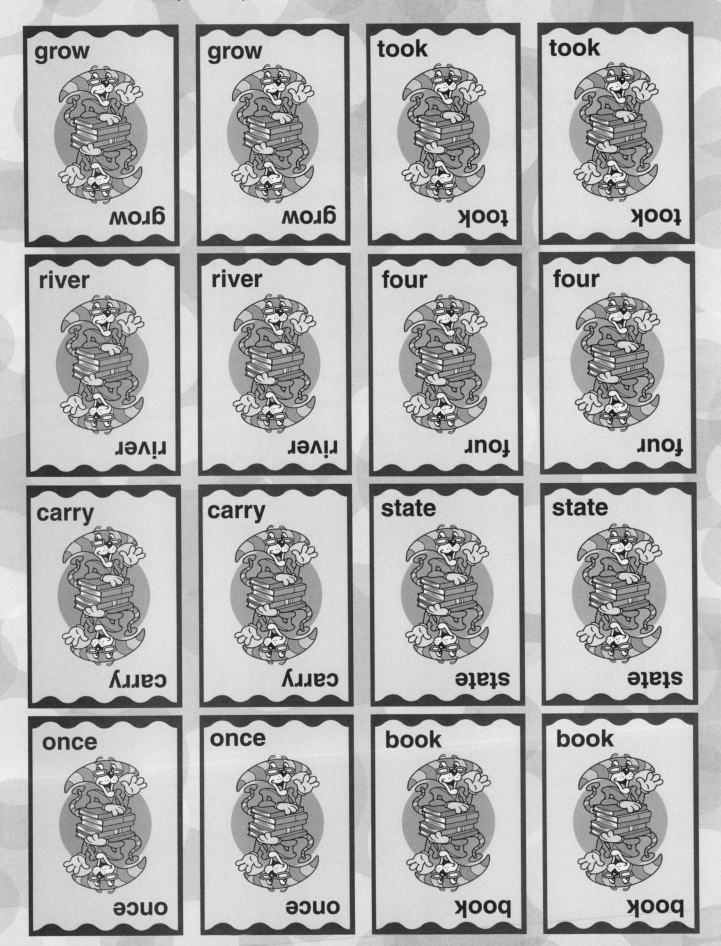

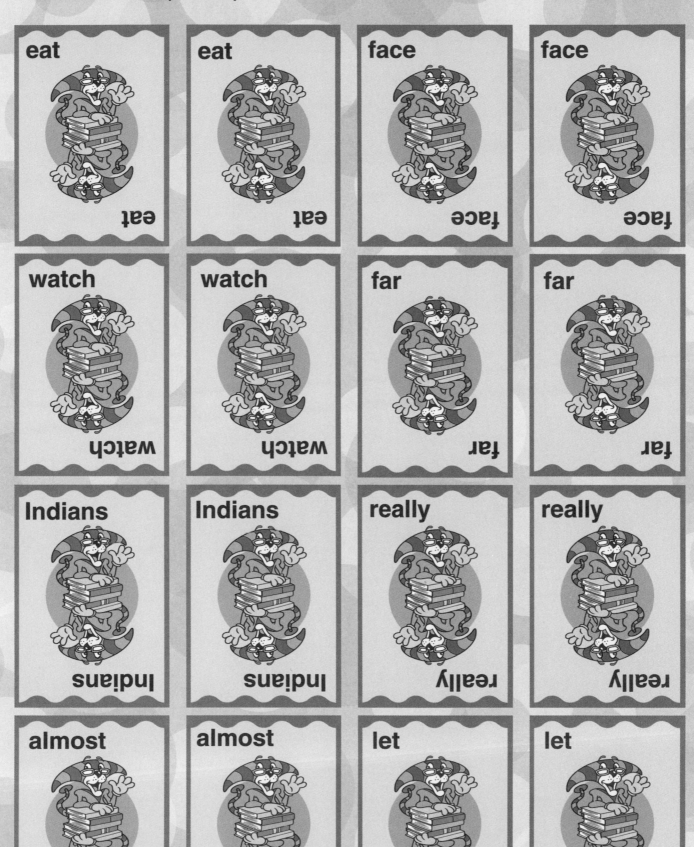

  (Teacher Created Resources)

| above  above | above  above | girl  girl | girl  girl |
| --- | --- | --- | --- |
| sometimes  sometimes | sometimes  sometimes | mountains  mountains | mountains  mountains |
| cut  cut | cut  cut | young  young | young  young |
| talk  talk | talk  talk | soon  soon | soon  soon |

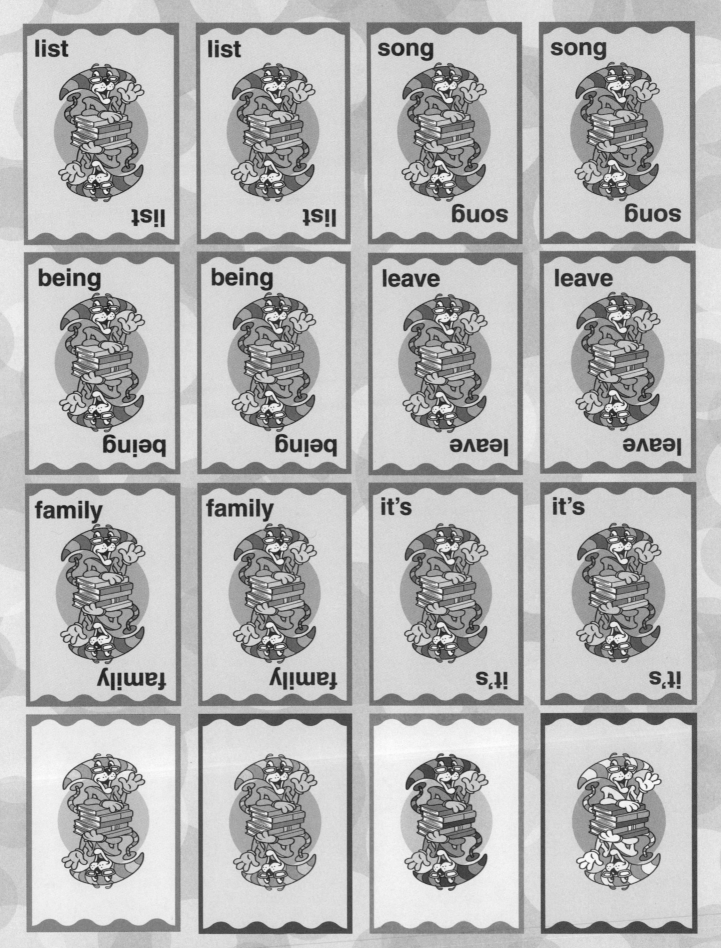

# Reference Charts

## Materials

- Picture Nouns Reference Charts (pages 171–173)
- Instant Words 151–300 Reference Chart (page 175)

## Teaching Suggestions

Below are teaching suggestions for the Picture Noun and Instant Words Reference Charts.

- *Wall Charts*—Post the charts on a wall for students to use as quick and easy references.

- *Partner Reading*—Place students in pairs. Make copies of a chart and have students practice reading the words to their partners.

- *Picture Noun Reading Practice*—Use a blank piece of paper or strip of paper to cover the pictures. Have the student try to read each word. To find out if he or she read it correctly, slip the paper down just one line to expose the picture. This gives instant feedback, provides motivation, and encourages self-teaching.

- *Picture Noun Writing Practice*—Use a blank piece of paper or strip of paper to cover a word. Have the student try to write the word. To find out if he or she wrote it correctly, slip the paper down just one line to expose the word. This gives instant feedback, provides motivation, and encourages self-teaching.

- *Oral Spelling Practice*—Place students in pairs. Have one student read the word from the chart while the other student tries to spell the word.

- *Independent Practice*—Use the worksheet on page 170. Have students write describing words for each of the listed Picture Nouns. (*Note:* If they are beginning writers and readers, you may choose to have students do only a few words each day. For a challenge, have students write sentences using their describing words and Picture Nouns.)

- *Creating Phrases and Sentences*—Have students write simple phrases and sentences using the words on the Instant Words and Picture Noun charts.

- *Sentence Building*—Make multiple copies of the charts and hand them out to students. Have them cut out the words and make sentences or phrases. Have students paste their sentences or phrases onto a sheet of paper and take them home to read to their parents.

- *Centers*—Post the charts in centers and create your own activities. For example, students can create their own stories using the words on the Instant Words and Picture Nouns charts.

- *Home Practice*—Send copies of the charts home for students to practice reading the words to their parents.

# Describing Picture Nouns

**Name:** _____     **Date:** _____

**Directions:** Write an adjective (describing word) for each Picture Noun.

**Example:** _fuzzy_ rabbit

_____ pants          _____ man

_____ book           _____ crayon

_____ flower         _____ boat

_____ bird           _____ chair

_____ horse          _____ soup

_____ shoes          _____ juice

_____ field          _____ pen

_____ nurse          _____ cloud

_____ pear           _____ movie

# Picture Nouns

 **People**

| | |
|---|---|
| boy | girl |
| man | woman |
| baby | |

 **Toys**

| | |
|---|---|
| ball | doll |
| train | game |
| toy | |

 **Numbers 1–5**

| | |
|---|---|
| one | four |
| two | five |
| three | |

 **Clothing**

| | |
|---|---|
| shirt | pants |
| dress | shoes |
| hat | |

 **Pets**

| | |
|---|---|
| cat | dog |
| bird | fish |
| rabbit | |

 **Furniture**

| | |
|---|---|
| table | chest |
| chair | desk |
| sofa | |

 **Eating Objects**

| | |
|---|---|
| cup | fork |
| plate | spoon |
| bowl | |

 **Transportation**

| | |
|---|---|
| car | plane |
| truck | boat |
| bus | |

 **Food**

| | |
|---|---|
| bread | apple |
| meat | cereal |
| soup | |

 **Drinks**

| | |
|---|---|
| water | soda |
| milk | malt |
| juice | |

Teacher Created Resources

Teacher Created Resources

Teacher Created Resources

Teacher Created Resources

Teacher Created Resources

Teacher Created Resources

Teacher Created Resources

Teacher Created Resources

Teacher Created Resources

Teacher Created Resources

Teacher Created Resources

Teacher Created Resources

Teacher Created Resources

Teacher Created Resources

Teacher Created Resources

Teacher Created Resources

Teacher Created Resources

Teacher Created Resources

Teacher Created Resources

Teacher Created Resources

Teacher Created Resources

Teacher Created Resources

Teacher Created Resources

Teacher Created Resources

Teacher Created Resources

Teacher Created Resources

Teacher Created Resources

Teacher Created Resources

Teacher Created Resources

Teacher Created Resources

Teacher Created Resources

# Picture nouns

 **Numbers 6–10**

| | |
|---|---|
| six | nine |
| seven | ten |
| eight | |

 **Fruit**

| | |
|---|---|
| fruit | pear |
| orange | banana |
| grape | |

 **Plants**

| | |
|---|---|
| bush | plant |
| flower | tree |
| grass | |

 **Sky Things**

| | |
|---|---|
| sun | cloud |
| moon | rain |
| star | |

**Earth Things**

| | |
|---|---|
| lake | field |
| rock | hill |
| dirt | |

 **Farm Animals**

| | |
|---|---|
| horse | chicken |
| cow | duck |
| pig | |

 **Workers**

| | |
|---|---|
| farmer | doctor |
| cook | nurse |
| policeman | |

 **Entertainment**

| | |
|---|---|
| radio | television |
| movie | band |
| ball game | |

 **Writing Tools**

| | |
|---|---|
| pen | chalk |
| pencil | crayon |
| computer | |

 **Reading Things**

| | |
|---|---|
| magazine | sign |
| book | letter |
| newspaper | |

# Instant Words 151–300

| | | | |
|---|---|---|---|
| 151. set | 189. point | 227. left | 265. river |
| 152. put | 190. page | 228. don't | 266. four |
| 153. end | 191. letters | 229. few | 267. carry |
| 154. does | 192. mother | 230. while | 268. state |
| 155. another | 193. answer | 231. along | 269. once |
| 156. well | 194. found | 232. might | 270. book |
| 157. large | 195. study | 233. close | 271. hear |
| 158. must | 196. still | 234. something | 272. stop |
| 159. big | 197. learn | 235. seemed | 273. without |
| 160. even | 198. should | 236. next | 274. second |
| 161. such | 199. American | 237. hard | 275. later |
| 162. because | 200. world | 238. open | 276. miss |
| 163. turned | 201. high | 239. example | 277. idea |
| 164. here | 202. every | 240. beginning | 278. enough |
| 165. why | 203. near | 241. life | 279. eat |
| 166. asked | 204. add | 242. always | 280. face |
| 167. went | 205. food | 243. those | 281. watch |
| 168. men | 206. between | 244. both | 282. far |
| 169. read | 207. own | 245. paper | 283. Indians |
| 170. need | 208. below | 246. together | 284. really |
| 171. land | 209. country | 247. got | 285. almost |
| 172. different | 210. plants | 248. group | 286. let |
| 173. home | 211. last | 249. often | 287. above |
| 174. us | 212. school | 250. run | 288. girl |
| 175. move | 213. father | 251. important | 289. sometimes |
| 176. try | 214. keep | 252. until | 290. mountains |
| 177. kind | 215. trees | 253. children | 291. cut |
| 178. hand | 216. never | 254. side | 292. young |
| 179. picture | 217. started | 255. feet | 293. talk |
| 180. again | 218. city | 256. car | 294. soon |
| 181. change | 219. earth | 257. miles | 295. list |
| 182. off | 220. eyes | 258. night | 296. song |
| 183. play | 221. light | 259. walked | 297. being |
| 184. spell | 222. thought | 260. white | 298. leave |
| 185. air | 223. head | 261. sea | 299. family |
| 186. away | 224. under | 262. began | 300. it's |
| 187. animals | 225. story | 263. grow | |
| 188. house | 226. saw | 264. took | |